What They Won't Teach You In Grad School

◆ ◆ ◆ ◆ ◆ ◆ ◆

ADVANCE PRAISE FOR *WHAT THEY WON'T TEACH*

YOU IN GRAD SCHOOL

A must-read book for anyone ready to enter today's workforce or thinking about advancing in their career. It gives practical tips about what it takes to succeed in what will continue to be a highly competitive race to the top.

Yasmin Delahoussaye, Ed.D.
Retired College President

This is a must-do training program for education and law enforcement organizations to implement in response to our 21st century and beyond scenarios.

Bradley J. Young
Retired Law Enforcement Officer and Professor Emeritus

Dr. A is a gifted author who brilliantly delivers relevant facts and cogent information in a clear and relevant manner. Her new book, "What They Won't Teach You in Grad School," is a must-read for grad students looking for real guidance that actually works.

Parthenia Grant, Ph.D.
Best-selling author of I Thought I Was The Crazy One

What They Won't Teach You In Grad School

◆ ◆ ◆ ◆ ◆ ◆ ◆

Dr. Stephanie A. Atkinson-Alston

What They Won't Teach You In Grad School

Contents

Dedication

This book is dedicated to the many people who told me that I had a voice, a keen eye for observation, an honest perspective of the truth, and a heart for making a difference.

In memory of my dear friend, Lee P. Mahon, Ed. D.

To Big Mama/Sister Topps/Ethel Mae Madkin, I always believed that if I could be half the woman you were, I would be a good woman. Thank you for everything!

Love,

Ann

Acknowledgment

I acknowledge that I have been called to my vocation by someone bigger than me.

About the Author

Dr. Stephanie A. Atkinson-Alston is an entrepreneur, professional development, and leadership evidence-based coach. As the Director of An Atkinson Alston Production, she engages clients through coaching to move them to their desired goals. Through observations as an entrepreneur, decorated retired Navy veteran, post-secondary educator, and college administrator, Dr. Atkinson-Alston confidentially guides clients to promote partnerships and develop robust resources.

She possesses an evidence-based coaching certification from Fielding Graduate University and is a member of the International Coaching Federation (ICF).

You want to hone your performance so that it becomes a part of you and is sincere and real.

CHAPTER 1

Each Journey Begins with a Single Step, Or at Least an Interview

❖ ❖ ❖ ❖ ❖ ❖ ❖ ❖

T rey and Felicia are pursuing their career in higher education in different ways. Trey recently received his Bachelor of Science degree in Psychology and would now like to pursue a master's degree so that he can become a faculty member at his local community college.

Felicia has been a division chair at her university for the past dozen years. Feeling stale in the position, she aspires to become a dean at the school. She looks at the career advancement as a way to help solve current campus issues as well as increasing her retirement fund.

These two scenarios are very common in higher education. While different, the process for each individual to realize their goal is the same. In fact, this premise holds true for anyone looking to change jobs at their academic institution or if they are looking to move on to another school.

Careful preparation on each step of the journey can often make the difference between receiving a job offer, or receiving the dreaded, "While your qualifications were impressive, we have decided on someone else to fulfill the position of _____." To avoid that outcome, we are going to travel along Trey and Felicia's journey. We will pursue each step of the process, and you can apply the lessons to your own efforts. I gleaned my knowledge on this subject from going through this myself and working with others who have done the same.

The assumption is that you have prepared a dynamic resume with all the pertinent qualifications to match the position you are going for at your school or another. It worked because you got your foot in the door. That is the job of a resume. It is not going to get you the job you covet, but it will enable you to state your case for the position through the interview process.

Initially, I believe that a person has to understand and realize what skill sets and traits they bring to the table. It is funny how so many of us have an instinctive feel for what we can contribute to a position, but we never take the time to think them through thoroughly. It is well worth the time to review your abilities and list them. Abilities are everything from the technical knowledge you have to perform the job you want, to some of those subjective traits like "get along well with people." It is also a good idea to list those traits you feel that you lack. This is not to share in the interview, but to help you better match up to a position. It also enables you to know what skills or knowledge you need to improve on.

Without knowing this fundamental information about yourself, you are going to have difficulty knowing how you can marry your skills to a potential job. That is because the next step is to take that knowledge of what you can do and analyze how it can help the school or position you are applying for. Remember, the school is hiring someone to fulfill a need they have. You want to show how you can fill that need and aid the school in moving forward.

At the end of the day, your new school or supervisor must be happy with the things you can do for them when you begin your job on the first day and in the future. Likewise, you need to make sure the position you seek will be viable for you over the next ten years or so. For this reason, I advocate that you do as much research as possible on a job that seems to be the best fit for you. With the ability to do extensive online research on any school and their open positions, you can certainly track down the best fit for yourself. For one thing, when you know that on paper the job you are looking at seems close to ideal, the enthusiasm you bring to the interview for it will be tangible. Those conducting interviews like to see that quality, and genuine enthusiasm shines through in an interview.

An added benefit of your research is that you will show the interviewer that you are aware of the structure and hierarchy of the school as well as the school's positive attributes and those things they are trying to accomplish. With this information, you can tailor your answers to showing how you can help the school reach new goals it has set for itself. You want to be able to walk into the interview as a problem solver, specifically for the issues the school faces.

Knowing about the school and how you can best serve it is paramount. Equally important is preparing how you will answer questions to show this knowledge. Being able to articulate your responses to questions is equally important. I call this taking your research to the next level. Think about how a person takes what they learned in their degree and apply it to a practical situation. As an example, an accounting major graduates with a degree in that subject, but the real test is the first time she is asked to audit a company's books. That new accountant has to take the facts and theory learned in school and then apply it successfully to the real world.

Preparing for your interview is no different. Most people can make an educated guess on a majority of questions they will receive and prepare accordingly. Those who are thoroughly prepared for an interview know enough about the school and the position they are applying for that they'll be able to take questions and tailor their answers to how it will best help the school. The goal here is that not only are you saying to the interviewer that you are the best person for the job, but you are illustrating through your knowledge that you can back up that claim.

As for some practical tips on how to go about the necessary research, go to the school's website. Start with the "Home" tab and systematically go through the entire site, even if parts of it do not pertain to the position you want. For example, you might not even be interested in sports; it might be important to the school, and you want to be able to talk about it with confidence. Too many people become so focused on the position they want that they fail to look at the college they are applying to as an organic whole.

If the school's website posts them, pay special attention to any documents that talk about the school's mission and vision. Completely study any strategic plans they might have posted. Information from these areas will give you a clear idea of where the college is moving toward and if it fits in with what you are seeking. Also important when doing any research on a higher education institution is their accreditation. Their accreditation documents give a sense of anything the college might need to address or fix in order to stay compliant with accreditation criteria.

Another source of information that can be helpful is if the college is conducting any type of capital campaign. Most schools have fundraising campaigns going on all the time. Capital campaigns are very specific in the goals that are set and, more importantly, how the money raised is designated. For example, a campaign designed to build a new science center shows that science is a priority of the school. Raising funds to upgrade the school's library and making it more accessible via internet for students and outside users show a desire to be top of the line in technology, and to be able to serve more people. The same can be said of schools doing capital campaigns to build facilities and infrastructure to do more coursework online. These are schools who want to be relevant and are actively competing with other good schools doing the same thing.

All of this extensive preliminary work is going to show you as an expert on the school and how what you bring to the open position will benefit the school. In the initial interview, you want to position yourself as a person who understands the school and its expectations. You want to show how your skill set will enable the school to reach that next level that it aspires to attain.

You might have heard of the 7 P's – Proper Prior Planning Prevents Pitifully Poor Performance. Nothing is truer than when prepping for your interview. It is one thing to know all about the school, the position, what you can bring the job, etc., but it is quite another to be able to bring it out at the interview.

Let's talk for a minute about knowing your strengths and weaknesses. I admire those who can study a topic and articulate on it for a half hour as if they were experts. I am not talking about those who are fudging it, but the people who can learn something quickly and intelligently talk about it. If you are one of those, then being ready for the interview will be easy.

Unfortunately, this is not most of us. Most people need to prepare themselves for the interview. Let's assume you did all your research. You know everything you can find out about the school and the job. You can mentally prepare the answers in your mind, but nothing beats the actual practice of saying what you know. Like an actor preparing for a part or a good speaker getting ready for a presentation, nothing will be better than if you practice what you want to say.

When called for an interview, it is okay to ask about the format. Are you talking to one person or five? And if it is five, are you sitting in front of the group or will it be five different individual interviews? There is a chance the first interview will be a screening interviewer and how you do there will determine if you come back to speak before a larger group.

Whatever the case, you will have to give a bit of history on yourself — background, schooling, education, job experience, etc. Know what you want to share about yourself in the interview and practice it. Even if you do not have the opportunity to say it all at once, thoroughly understanding what you want others to know about you will help you answer questions on that topic as they come up.

As for practicing answers specific to the school and the position you want, find someone to practice with whether it be a mentor, friend, or family member. If it is someone familiar with interviewing others for openings, let them take their best shot at you. For others, think through some logical questions you might be asked and give that to them as a starting point. One thing about using family and friends is that they can be brutal; let them. They care about you and have your best interests at heart. They want you to be prepared. The odds are good if you survive their interview, the real one will be easy.

Constantly evaluate and appraise your performance in these practice sessions as well as asking for feedback. You want to hone your performance so that it becomes a part of you and is sincere and real. What might seem artificial at the beginning of practicing for an interview will eventually become authentic as you mindfully apply yourself to the task.

You want to be genuine. All you are doing by practicing is getting comfortable in articulating what you know and why you are the perfect fit for the job you are going after. Sometimes we need a little work to put forth our best authentic selves.

While you can anticipate many questions at an interview, you are going to be hit with something that you might not be comfortable with, and you are not sure what to do. Don't let it throw you. For example, I have applied for positions where those conducting an interview asked me to write an impromptu short paper on a topic. This is not my strong suit. At this stage in life, I am comfortable talking with those conducting an interview, but this was something that made me nervous. To get over my anxiety, I would practice my writing along the lines interviewers have asked me in the past. Perhaps writing would never come up in an interview again, but if it did, I was as prepared to tackle that task as I could be.

Summary

Preparation is the key to any interview situation. You need to know yourself well, know the company (or school for our purposes) as thoroughly as you can, and know what you can bring to help that school be more successful. You are the problem solver, and you are the best person to solve a particular problem of the school. That is the mindset to go in with to the interview and only knowing as many facts as possible will help you achieve the mindset. Preparation includes practicing for the interview. This can be anything from the old standby of practicing your answers in front of a mirror to role-playing the interview with others. Whatever occurs during a practice or in the interview itself, learn from it. You might not get the job you go after the first time, but every interview is a learning experience worth thousands of dollars that will make you more prepared the next time.

Complete the following sections for **"Each Journey Begins with a Single Step, or At Least An Interview"** *as it applies to your situation or career trajectory.*

REFLECTION:

How can you use what you've learned in this chapter to change or improve the current situation? How can you apply what you've learned for career advancement? Hint: You can request support from a friend, colleague, mentor to assist you!

_____
_____
_____
_____
_____
_____
_____
_____
_____
_____
_____
_____
_____
_____
_____
_____
_____
_____
_____
_____
_____
_____
_____
_____

ACTION STEPS:

List 1 or 2 action steps you intend to take starting today.

_____

_____

_____

_____

_____

_____

_____

_____

_____

_____

_____

_____

_____

_____

_____

_____

_____

_____

_____

_____

_____

_____

_____

_____

_____

_____

_____

ACTION CELEBRATION:

After completing the actions over a couple of weeks, celebrate yourself. Write down how you will celebrate. Hint: It could be as small as listening to your favorite song, watching a favorite TV show, going out for dinner or...

_____

_____

_____

_____

_____

_____

_____

_____

_____

_____

_____

_____

_____

_____

_____

_____

_____

_____

_____

_____

_____

_____

_____

_____

_____

Mindfulness is a deliberate choice on your part to live in the present where your heartfelt values guide your actions.

CHAPTER 2

Mindfulness in the Moment

❖ ❖ ❖ ❖ ❖ ❖ ❖ ❖

F elicia walked into her interview primed and ready to answer any question put to her. Having already been at the college for a while, she knew that she had more background on its goals and organization than anybody who would come in from the outside. Felicia also knew most of the people on the panel, and that gave her a degree of comfort. She was ready with what she was going to say. She was confident!

That lasted until a member of the search committee Felicia didn't know asked his first question. She had something in mind that she was going to say based on the previous question, but the one he asked seemed to come out of left field. She tried to bring into her answer what she was planning on saying anyway, but the result sounded half-hearted and lame. After that, it took Felicia a few more questions and responses before she felt like she was back on her game. Inside, though, she wondered if she had blown the interview.

Felicia's experience is not unusual. A person prepares for an interview and feels like they have total command of anything thrown at them. Then if the interview begins to go in a direction not foreseen, the interviewee can be completely flummoxed. Some people are terrific at getting back on track with an interview or a lesson or a speech when knocked off their stride. Others struggle to the end of the event as they try to recover. As I heard a senior military officer once put it, "Battle plans are great until the first shot is fired. Then you have to start improvising in conjunction with your set plan."

What I tell anyone going into an interview is that you have to approach it with a sincere state of mindfulness. Now mindfulness is certainly a word used in many different situations and contexts. Before I elaborate on how being mindful impacts your performance during an interview, let's look at the word and its meaning.

]Mindfulness is your ability to know yourself. Remember when I said in the last chapter that you wanted to present your authentic self to others in an interview? Exercising mindfulness is the way you achieve that authenticity. Mindfulness is a deliberate choice on your part to live in the present where your heartfelt values guide your actions. The other component of mindfulness is that you do all of this in a setting of nonjudgement. You aren't judging yourself or anyone else in any given situation.

When you can do this, the understanding you have of yourself will enable you to make good decisions based on who you really are. When you throw in the nonjudgement aspect, it is easier to know and work with your strengths and limitations. You become acutely aware of areas where you might be lacking. This is the first step in turning those weaknesses into a strength. For example, you might be terrible at public speaking. If this is going to be a detriment to advancement or securing your dream position, you are going to have to take steps to get help and become better in front of an audience. You might not ever be invited to give a "Ted Talk," but you are going to more than hold your own when it is time to give a speech. However, without first recognizing that as a weak point and how it could affect your future, you might not have gone the extra mile to become better at it.

Mindfulness helps you bring all of who you are to the table. I want to caution you about two things here. Making mindfulness an inherent part of you does not happen overnight nor is it a one and done deal. On the first part, it takes a conscious effort to become mindful. A person generally has to push him or herself to do this. However, by constantly being aware of being mindful and applying yourself each and every day, it will become a part of you. It is similar to making the decision that you are going to become a healthy eater; you might have many fits and starts in the beginning, especially if you think of French fries as a vegetable. However, the more you set your mind to achieving this and the more you do it, it doesn't take too long before you are making much healthier decisions at the food store or in a restaurant.

I think the hardest part of mindfulness is when you are attempting to use it as you are relating with other people. That is why it is so important to know yourself as well as you can. We are all influenced by others whether we know them or not. It could be anything that can throw us off. It could be their opinion, how they are talking, their past experience, or the really bad job they did assembling their wardrobe in the morning. This is where the nonjudgement comes in again. That nonjudgement filters through the nonessential aspects of what is going on around you or the other person, so you can focus in on what is important.

When it comes to the interview, that focus is what is important. When you are committed to being mindful of everything you do, it makes it easier for you to be a more aware human being. So many of us become so concerned with showing everything we know about the job and the organization and how our experience and knowledge will make us the best problem solver to hire, that we forget to listen to the questions!

There is the old adage that we have two ears and one mouth so that we should be listening twice as much as we speak. This is a good piece of advice in general, but very important when going through the interview process for a new position. All you have to do is watch the news on any given night to become frustrated with how many people, whether they be politicians, government officials, or almost anyone else, do not answer a direct question. While you have certain qualities that you want to share with the interviewers, you need to be patient and focus on the questions asked of you. Being mindful enables you to listen better to what a person is asking and, therefore, give a direct answer.

When you achieve mindfulness in any situation, it is easier to allow events to come to you. That is because you know yourself to the extent that you will respond in a way that reflects your values. In a way, nothing is more important than being able to do that in an interview. If it is a position you want, then you want to be offered it on the merits of who you are. This way, when you begin the job, you approach it with confidence because you didn't have to put on any false airs or exaggerate your ability during the interview.

We all go into an interview with a mental checklist of what we want to share. Don't worry if it doesn't all get out during the actual questions and answers. Almost any interview gives the job seeker an opportunity to say anything else that was not brought up during the questioning. Know you will get this chance at the end. Many times, we come into an interview feeling like a pitcher of water filled to the brim. We can't wait to start talking for fear we will spill all over the floor. Go in, focus on each person asking questions, and simply answer them. Everything you want to say will be shared in the end.

I think as an educator, it's extremely important to be

mindful. It will put you at the center of what's being said by others and allows you to respond accordingly. The questions you receive at an interview will give you a clear idea of what the college or organization is looking for in the candidates. If a college is asking questions revolving around accreditation, you know that is a hot topic for them. You can get a sense of where they are looking to go as a college or university. You can get a clear idea from what the interviewers ask you if on-line learning is one of their focal points.

Let's take this another step forward. You worked on your mindfulness. You did a great job being grounded in your interview and carefully listened to and answered what the selection panel asked you. They offered you the job! Now you can take that mindfulness and apply it to your new position. Mindfulness for any leadership position is a key to being an effective leader. You are going to be working with others, both above and below you, and you need to exercise that focus in any dealings you have with them. The same principles apply as they did in the interview. When trying to solve a problem, you have to have a clear idea of the issue that you have to tackle.

Mindfulness energizes you to clearly listen to others and read any information regarding the problem. You can then clearly look at various options and select the best one in accord with your values. Those people you work with or manage will know that you are someone that will listen to them when they come to you with an issue. Over time, they will also come to realize that your decision-making dovetails with who you are. This is how a leader gains respect from subordinates, superiors, and peers.

Once in your new position, constantly work at your mindfulness and being authentic. I'm currently in an organization where things in the past have bogged people down.

As their leader, I need to know a little bit about the past, and then reassure them that the shortcomings of the past are not going to lead us to the future. It is all about building trust and respect among all of us because that helps folks to be successful.

When it comes to becoming more mindful, it is about being present. Sometimes, it is as simple as putting both feet on the floor, feeling the ground, and taking what time and opportunity brings you. I was in a meeting just this past week, and a colleague brought up a subject that I kind of wish he hadn't. Once he did, how was I supposed to address that?

I looked directly at the person, tuned out everything around me, and mindfully listened to him. After that, I re-iterated some points he made, and we brought in another colleague who was also involved in this particular issue. Together, we hashed out a solution. If I was intent on doing something else when this man first approached me instead of making a conscious effort to listen to his problem and try to solve it, then it might have festered and become worse over time. I mindfully decided to listen to him and then mindfully decided to see if we could work out a solution.

Don't think I am a master at mindfulness. I have gotten so much better at it over time, but it is something I consistently work on and remind myself to exercise. I don't think we ever come to the end of finding out more about ourselves every day. By working on mindfulness, you will know who you are, which will only help you be better at interviews or doing your job.

Summary

Mindfulness allows you to embrace both your positive qualities and those you need to work on, giving you a clear picture of who you are. It helps you know how you will act in any given situation. This quality allows you to be at your best in any situation, whether it be in an interview for a position or when you are working hard in your job. Mindfulness enables you to focus in on people and situations to help you make clear, confident decisions.

*Complete the following sections for **"Mindfulness in the Moment"** as it applies to your situation or career trajectory.*

REFLECTION:

How can you use what you've learned in this chapter to change or improve the current situation? How can you apply what you've learned for career advancement? Hint: You can request support from a friend, colleague, mentor to assist you!

_____
_____
_____
_____
_____
_____
_____
_____
_____
_____
_____
_____
_____
_____
_____
_____
_____
_____
_____
_____
_____
_____
_____
_____

ACTION STEPS:

List 1 or 2 action steps you intend to take starting today.

_____

_____

_____

_____

_____

_____

_____

_____

_____

_____

_____

_____

_____

_____

_____

_____

_____

_____

_____

_____

_____

_____

_____

_____

_____

_____

_____

ACTION CELEBRATION:

After completing the actions over a couple of weeks, celebrate yourself. Write down how you will celebrate. Hint: It could be as small as listening to your favorite song, watching a favorite TV show, going out for dinner or...

_____
_____
_____
_____
_____
_____
_____
_____
_____
_____
_____
_____
_____
_____
_____
_____
_____
_____
_____
_____
_____
_____
_____
_____

Millennials' openness to mentoring,
authentic leadership and coaching
helps them shift their career path
in the direction they want to go.

CHAPTER 3

Millennials in the Workforce

❖ ❖ ❖ ❖ ❖ ❖ ❖ ❖

T rey walked into his new office. It was the size of a broom closet, and he shared it with another Teacher's Assistant, but he felt good when he sat at the small desk for the first day. He did well in his interview, and the university accepted him into its Master's Program for Psychology. He had done very well throughout the interview process. It was more involved for him than some other students because he was also applying for financial assistance. This meant being a TA for one of the psychology professors.

Sharon Watson took him on, and one of the introductory psych classes she taught to the undergrads consisted of two lectures a week. She taught these, but there was a third class each week where the large lecture class was broken down into five smaller groups taught by a Teacher's Assistant. Trey was one of those TAs who also had to be available to the students in his class when they had questions and concerns. Now that he had been on the job for two weeks, he found that he enjoyed the classroom assignment, but he wasn't crazy about having office hours, waiting for students to come to him. He wondered if he could talk to Professor Watson about making some changes.

Trey's story is a familiar one that I see in some of the younger people working in a college setting. To be clear, I am specifically talking about Millennials. The criteria to be a Millennial is to be born somewhere between 1981-1996. As

I write this book in 2018, I am talking about anyone who is between 22 and 37 years old. Those that fit into this category are the next generation that will be leading colleges, companies, and organizations in the very near future if they are not doing so already.

I am what is known as a Baby Boomer. We are workers who have been in the workforce for a long time and could be anywhere from heading up a business, organization, or department to winding down toward retirement. In today's economy and environment, people work longer than they used to — some because they want to and others because they have to keep working.

This chapter is not about who is better at their jobs, because the world does not work that way. Each person brings certain talents, knowledge, and passions to a position. It doesn't matter if they are a Baby Boomer, a Millennial, or that group of people that sits in between the two: Generation X. However, I do want to focus on some tendencies that I see in Millennials because if you are in this group and recognize what I am talking about, you will be in a better position to adjust your work ethic to help you carve out that career you want.

As Trey did in the story at the beginning of the chapter, many Millennials are very good at research and preparing themselves for an interview. Millennials are the first generation to grow up with computers, the internet, and much of the technology we take for granted today. Between knowing how to conduct a search and investigating social media, those in this age group are quite adept at pulling together information on the college they want to work for and the people who might be interviewing them. If they mindfully apply this knowledge and are aware of all that is going on in the interview, they have a good chance of winning the position they applied for with the school.

This is all fine and good; in fact, congratulations! However, one of the difficulties I have seen in Millennials is that they treat getting the position as if they crossed the finish line. It isn't the finish line; it is more like the five-mile mark in a marathon. That means there are 21 miles, 385 yards to go. Getting the job is great. Now, you must do the job.

When entering into the interview process, most places give a candidate a detailed job description of the position. This is especially true in academia. As a side note, if you are not given one, ask! If where you are interviewing at cannot provide one, it is probably a good idea to get out of there!

When you do have a job description in hand, study it thoroughly. I see too many Millennials who take on a job and then say, "I don't want to do this…" The "this" could be one aspect of the position or several. We all have certain things in our jobs we would rather not do. It is one thing if you didn't know about them, but when it is something that is clearly in the job description you read before taking on the job, then "I don't want to do this" comes across as whiny and is not going to endear you to your colleagues and supervisors.

Many Millennials take on the attitude of Trey. They rationalize that since they do not want to do something that is part of the job, then they have the right to try to bargain their way out of that duty or responsibility. I have done research and writing on the subject of Millennials, and there is a tendency to believe that this age group feels a sense of entitlement. Many factors go into this conclusion. A great deal has to do with how parents and teachers treated this group as they grew up. I have to admit that it goes as far as how some colleges interact with their undergrads.

Whatever psychological factors contribute to this sense of entitlement, it comes as a rude awakening to some people that the world is not quite as easy once you leave the friendly confines of being a student to entering the workforce. Don't get me wrong; there are exceptions. I find young people who worked while they were in high school and college have a better ability at transitioning into working for a school than those that never worked before. What I want to do here is impress on everyone that when you first take on a job, you are expected to do the job that you were hired for by the school or company. You impressed them! They thought you would be a good fit. Many times that means taking on the bad with the good.

It is a good chance for the Millennial to learn if this is a job that they want to do 3, 5, or 15 years down the road. I will be the first to say that sometimes the job we fight hard to get might not meet our expectations. It happens. My suggestion for that is to make the best out of the situation until you can make a change. In the meantime, analyze what you do like and don't like about the position. This will be valuable information as you shape your career in the future.

I do not suggest that you take a position going in with the perception that you will change those aspects of the job you do not find acceptable. In general, the world does not work like that. If you take a job and immediately don't do the duties you do not like or actively push to change them right away, you aren't going to make many friends. Please note that whether you are in academia, business, or the nonprofit world, the positive networking that you do where you work is as important as any networking you do on the outside. We never know when someone might be a key to our future later in our career.

Did you ever hear the saying, "Rome wasn't built in a day?" It means that you have to exercise patience. The wise young person takes this approach when starting their new job. If they really want to make a difference where they are at, they will do what is expected of them. However, they are also taking that experience, the good and bad, and planning how to make their position better. When you can go to a supervisor with a firm plan in hand that would make your position even more effective, he or she is more apt to listen. If you can figure out how to do that and eliminate some of your more distasteful duties, then it is a win-win!

I believe this helps Millenials focus on an area where they can not only make the best out of their job but also to thrive. It has to do with the planning process that a person needs to be successful in any job. If you were like Trey, who went from getting a bachelor's degree to working at a college, you had most of your undergrad days planned out. Every course had a syllabus with deadlines and all your steps spelled out to be successful in that class. The working world does not quite operate that way. Often, you are the one who has to make a plan filled with checkpoints and deadlines in order to be successful. You might also discover that more is on your shoulders when you advance in position.

This is why a school hired you. It is up to you to show initiative and organize your work in a way to meet the goals that you either set or that the school gave you. A few people have a natural talent for planning and organization. They are like the folks who never had a music lesson but can play any instrument. For most people, it takes practice and training. If this is a weak point for you, don't be afraid to seek out resources to get better at organization. If you read an idea that seems like it will work for you, mindfully apply that lesson.

I actually had a Millennial once tell me, "We're Millennials. We don't know how to do that organization stuff." I kid you not. The problem was that while she was truthful, she was also implying that since she didn't know how to implement organizational skills, then it wasn't all that important to learn. A wise person (and a successful one) knows what they don't know, and then goes out to overcome that deficiency.

I believe that Millennials come into the workforce with a great education and the resources and knowledge to take an accelerated career path no matter the career. However, they are slower to take the time and make an effort to navigate the practicalities of a new job so that they can excel in their position. No matter the generation, once you are in the workforce, nothing just "happens." A young man or woman has to work hard at doing what is expected of them and then putting themselves in a position to move on to the next rung of their career ladder.

Until you are the one in charge, your career is going to be one of adapting and working within the rules of wherever you are employed. Some working environments are better to work in than others. That is a factor to weigh when deciding if you want to work for a specific institution. I am not saying you should not be looking to make your mark where you work. That is the sign of someone who wants to be successful. However, do it within the context of where your job is. Learn what has been done in the past and what the future goals of the organization are. Use that knowledge and the experience you acquire every day to plan how to make things better. Put it on paper, present it to your supervisor, and if accepted, get out there and implement it!

Then you will be taking control of your career. Never expect somebody to hand it to you!

Summary

While Millennials are the next generation of leaders through all institutions in America, they have to acquire a better work ethic to effectively reach that next level. By approaching their work situation with mindfulness, they can learn and apply the necessary skills to propel them on the career path that they desire.

*Complete the following sections for "**Millennials in the Workforce**" as it applies to your situation or career trajectory.*

REFLECTION:

How can you use what you've learned in this chapter to change or improve the current situation? How can you apply what you've learned for career advancement? Hint: You can request support from a friend, colleague, mentor to assist you!

_____

_____

_____

_____

_____

_____

_____

_____

_____

_____

_____

_____

_____

_____

_____

_____

_____

_____

_____

_____

_____

_____

_____

_____

_____

ACTION STEPS:

List 1 or 2 action steps you intend to take starting today.

_____
_____
_____
_____
_____
_____
_____
_____
_____
_____
_____
_____
_____
_____
_____
_____
_____
_____
_____
_____
_____
_____
_____
_____

ACTION CELEBRATION:

After completing the actions over a couple of weeks, celebrate yourself. Write down how you will celebrate. Hint: It could be as small as listening to your favorite song, watching a favorite TV show, going out for dinner or...

_____

_____

_____

_____

_____

_____

_____

_____

_____

_____

_____

_____

_____

_____

_____

_____

_____

_____

_____

_____

_____

_____

_____

_____

Self-esteem issues are very much at the root of a toxic work environment.

CHAPTER 4

Toxic Work Environment

❖ ❖ ❖ ❖ ❖ ❖ ❖

Felicia looked up as she heard a knock on her door. She saw Roger During scowling at her. He worked in the same department she did at the university. They were peers with different responsibilities but reported to the same supervisor.

"Can I come in?" he asked. "I have a problem with what you said at the staff meeting."

Felicia got up and said, "Not right now, Roger. I have a meeting to get to. Besides, anything you want to say, I'd rather we do it with Stacy in the room." Stacy Upbridge was their boss.

"Well, I don't like what you said about my program today. You think that just because you flash your legs at the Dean that you can say anything you want!"

Felicia stood nose to nose with Roger. "First, Roger, I was suggesting a modification to the program that would help the students. Why do you have to take everything so personally? Second, I am a woman and dresses are appropriate office wear. You say one more comment like that to me, and I will report you for sexual harassment."

"So, you don't have the guts to talk this out with me?" he said, his face getting red.

"It is not an issue of guts, Roger. It is an issue of me not wasting my time." With that, Felicia firmly closed her door and walked down *the hallway and out of the building. As she strolled over to the office where she had a meeting, she was fuming. Looking at her watch, she saw she was going to be early for her appointment. She sat on a bench and took out her phone. She quickly composed an email and sent it over to Stacy Upbridge detailing the encounter she just had with Roger During. She knew from experience that it was important to document any such encounter.*

All jobs have their challenges. One of the hardest to deal with are those problems that have to do with the people you come into contact with in your position. Whether you are talking about supervisors, your staff that reports to you, or colleagues, the attitudes of other people can be the trickiest problem to overcome. I like to think I go into every day with an upbeat attitude and an excitement that this is a day where I am going to do a lot of good. Then I meet someone who can bring all that down with a negative word or attitude.

The negative people in the workplace bring about a toxic environment that is very hard to overcome. They can broadcast that negative attitude in so many ways. An individual can cast doubt on any new idea, especially if it isn't his or hers. I remember entering a new position determined to bring some new energy to my assignment. At the first meeting, I expressed some new ideas, and one of my new colleagues started talking about how they would never work. He talked about how things had been done for the past fifteen years and implied I was going to rock the boat too much. This reactionary attitude is common when others feel threatened by a newcomer.

Being mindful of being present in the moment, I went over to that person after the meeting. I told him, "I wasn't here fifteen years ago, but I am here now, and my pledge to you is to move us forward." I then threw out some suggestions on how this person could help me. I was fortunate that

I turned a possible obstacle into an ally on day one. I'm not sure if this individual felt threatened by the "new kid on the block" or if that was his nature. However, we worked together well after that.

I do not doubt that I could write an entire book on the problems of a toxic environment in the workplace. There are many emotional and psychological reasons why certain people you work with might bring a dark pall over the workplace. You also have different ways to deal with such a situation depending on the people and situation. It never hurts to try and talk with someone who is either directing their negative energy at you or the workplace in general. I have been in situations where I have talked to someone and found that a personal issue in their life was making them lash out at work. It doesn't mean what they did was right, but you might be in the position to help them or at least point them in a positive direction.

Then there are those who walk around like Eeyore of Winnie the Pooh fame. He was the donkey with a perpetual dark cloud hanging over him and was consistently downcast. This is a contagious personality trait. I realized it early in my career when a colleague who I liked a great deal left the office where we worked for a new job. Almost immediately it seemed that an aura of doom and gloom rose off the office. He and I never had any personality conflicts; in fact, we were friends. However, when he left, the workplace became more positive. It brought to mind the saying that some people brighten a room when they enter it; others when they leave!

A toxic environment can arise when a person feels threatened in their job. Whether the threat is real or perceived, it can greatly affect that person's actions. They tend to disagree with the ideas of anybody else or they are always insistent on things being done their way. Self-esteem issues are very much at the root of a toxic work environment. Most people seem to work from a place of fear. They have a fear of not being good enough in their job, they doubt their ability, and rather than setting out on a positive program of self-improvement and confidence, they direct their energy out in a negative way against others. Supervisors can also be a cause of the toxic work environment. A good manager coaches and guides his or her people in a positive way through encouragement and heading off an issue before they become a problem. Bad ones seem to enjoy chaos and to sow seeds of mistrust amongst their staff. They believe pitting one against the other is the best way to motivate others and meet the goals of the office or department. Let me say here that this does not work. At best, a manager might get positive short-term results, but it is not effective as morale bottoms out and the supervisor wonders why there are so many people always coming and going in the department.

Identifying the sources of a toxic environment is not always easy. Of course, it is not a problem when a person is publicly outspoken and shows their negative inclinations. Other people project negativity in subtler ways. Here is where you need to look at the micro-aggressive behavior of people. Originally, "micro-aggression" was a term that came in vogue in the 1970s to describe small casual verbal and behavioral indignities against people of color. Now it encompasses the intentional and unintentional slights against any person or group.

Through observation, you can tell when a person has something against an individual, or a certain group of people based on age, race, religion, etc. Unfortunately, with some people, they can have a large variety of criteria by which they look down on or feel threatened by a certain demographic. An older worker might have an immediate reaction against Millennials because he or she looks at them as a threat to their job. Others direct their ire at people of a different race or gender.

Micro-aggressive behavior can be anything from making a sneer when someone is talking or in more public displays of opposition when in a meeting. You can also gather micro-aggressive tendencies from how someone words and email or even a social media post. Other times, it might not be in how a person interacts with you, but by the fact that they avoid or ignore you entirely.

This all takes a mindful observation on your part. It pays to spend some time studying how someone interacts with you and identifying their micro-aggressions. Determine if it is directed solely at you or against an entire group of people of which you are a part. When you do that, you have a better idea of how to deal with the person. You do have a responsibility to deal with it, both for yourself and the sake of the workplace. Micro-aggressive behavior can be like a snowball you see in a cartoon. The snowball is dropped at the top of a hill and gathers size and momentum as it rolls down a hill before it smashes and demolishes something at the bottom. In this case, it is you or your workplace that gets demolished with the impact.

How you deal with the situation will vary with the circumstances. Whatever the case, document what is going on to strengthen your case later. Our memories are not always as solid as we would like. However, if you take five minutes and write down what just happened, that information is going to have more validity if you have a confrontation with the person in front of a supervisor. Facts you wrote down as they happened gives your cause more integrity than saying, "A couple of months ago, Tom said something at a meeting that did not make me look good."

As Felicia did in the opening story of this chapter, she quickly let her supervisor know what was going on when Roger came to see her. Sometimes we straddle a fine line between protecting ourselves and being a "snitch." It is always good to talk with a supervisor early in your relationship to determine how they want you to handle such situations if they arise. Hopefully, you work somewhere that is in harmony, and this is never a problem. However, it is good to know your workplace's policy on handling conflict.

A final word here on being a woman in the workplace. We live in a time where there is a great deal of focus on men harassing women at work. The "Me Too" movement has cast light on this ongoing situation. While it mainly showed the abuses of men toward women in the entertainment and high-level corporate environs, do not think for a moment that it has eliminated sexual harassment at work. The line in the opening story where Roger comments on Felicia "flashing her legs at the Dean" is a case in point. I dress professionally at work, but that might mean dresses and other feminine attributes to my clothes. I am feminine, and I am comfortable dressing that way. It doesn't mean it gives a man the license to comment on it in a lewd way.

As a woman, you are going to run into many micro-aggressions from men. Then again, some are not going to be all that micro. There is no place for this in the workplace or anywhere, for that matter. Because of the heightened interest against such behavior at work, do not be afraid to use that to your advantage if you are encountering harassment or abuse because of your gender. I am not sure if it will happen in my lifetime, but if we ever get men and women equal in the workplace in terms of salary, respect, and leadership positions, the workplace will have a lot less minefields for women to negotiate during their career.

Summary

A toxic environment in the workplace can bring down individuals or the work environment as a whole faster than any other obstacles. Individuals are the root cause of a toxic environment, and it can easily spread like a contagious disease. For the sake of a person's career and happiness at work, it pays for them to observe the actions of others for micro-aggressive behaviors and take appropriate action to bring them to a halt.

Complete the following sections for ***"Toxic Work Environment"*** *as it applies to your situation or career trajectory.*

REFLECTION:

How can you use what you've learned in this chapter to change or improve the current situation? How can you apply what you've learned for career advancement? Hint: You can request support from a friend, colleague, mentor to assist you!

_____

_____

_____

_____

_____

_____

_____

_____

_____

_____

_____

_____

_____

_____

_____

_____

_____

_____

_____

_____

_____

_____

_____

ACTION STEPS:

List 1 or 2 action steps you intend to take starting today.

ACTION CELEBRATION:

After completing the actions over a couple of weeks, celebrate yourself. Write down how you will celebrate. Hint: It could be as small as listening to your favorite song, watching a favorite TV show, going out for dinner or...

_____

_____

_____

_____

_____

_____

_____

_____

_____

_____

_____

_____

_____

_____

_____

_____

_____

_____

_____

_____

_____

_____

_____

Sometimes experience is a nicer way of saying that you gained insight from messing up.

CHAPTER 5

Management by Messing Up

◆ ◆ ◆ ◆ ◆ ◆ ◆

*W*alking into the office, Trey cringed as Dr. Roberts came up to him. Lydia Roberts was the assistant head of the department and in charge of the Teacher's Assistants. The semester was coming to an end, and Trey thought he was doing a decent job. An encounter with Dr. Roberts usually shattered that perception. Today was proving no exception.

Without a word of greeting, Dr. Roberts started right in on him. "Trey, there is only a week of the semester left before finals. I asked all the assistants to increase their office hours to offer extra help to the undergrads for the next two weeks. Why haven't you done that yet?"

"I did, Dr. Roberts," protested Trey. "When we had the meeting discussing the matter, I immediately wrote down the hours I could do and handed it to you."

"Trey, how many times have I told all of you that I take all notes, questions, and whatever through e-mail? It is the easiest way for me to keep track of everything going on around here."

Looking a little distressed, Trey said, "You are, right. You did tell us that. I thought I was efficient by giving you the information right away."

Dr. Roberts gave Trey a rare smile. "I know you told me you hope to teach at the college level. You know your stuff, but you need to follow protocol wherever you work. One thing I found out early on in my career is that there is never one protocol. It differs by school, and then you have to factor in how your supervisors do things. In academia, you need to follow the rules wherever you are. It is the nature of the beast, and sometimes the best way to learn is to keep in mind your mistakes, learn from them, and let it be a learning experience on what you are supposed to do."

Trey's experience is something anybody who works in a college setting, or almost any business or organization, runs into. There is going to be a time where you are going to mess up something that you are doing in your job. Honestly, it is going to be more than once. Nobody is perfect, and every institution has its own rules and at times, idiosyncrasies, that an employee has to follow. There are also going to be situations that arise where the initial decision you make might not be the best one.

There are reasons that more advanced positions and titles look for experience on the part of the applicant in addition to education. Having experience means you have navigated the everyday problems and conflicts that arise in a job. You might encounter brand new problems in your new position, but the assumption is that you know how to deal with setbacks and obstacles.

Sometimes experience is a nicer way of saying that you gained insight from messing up. It is especially true when you are in a management position. While you need to know the process in your institution or organization, being a manager means you will be working with people. When you throw in that dynamic to any job, the possibilities of problems become compounded. Now you are also working with someone's else's personality and their place on the learning curve.

From my experience and observation, many of my colleagues begin to deal with their new management role by messing up when they receive a promotion into positions where they might not possess all the skills necessary. Often, the need to improve or acquire certain skills only becomes evident when the rubber meets the road, and a person starts the new job. Unfortunately, the spotlight shines on needed skills when you mess up. Hopefully, it is only a small glitch in your work, but it could be something bigger. While you need to evaluate how much you messed up, the most important concept is how you respond to messing up!

There is a saying that the only way to be successful is to have failures. This is not as counterintuitive as you might first think. Nobody goes through any job without something going wrong. Rather than getting depressed and beating yourself up over the negative, use it as a learning opportunity. It is important to look honestly at what went wrong. Sometimes things go wrong for reasons beyond our control. These tend to be in the minority. If something happens under our watch, then we have a degree of responsibility. It is vital to analyze mindfully what went wrong and to figure out how to avoid the same thing happening again in the future.

A component of "mindfulness" is to look at a situation without judgment. Many managers can be harder on themselves than they ever are on other people. This is something you do not have the time for when you are trying to make the best out of something going wrong. Accept your responsibility for what you did that might have contributed to the situation and then move on!

When you break down how you might have done better to avoid messing up, you must focus on whatever you did incorrectly. You might see what skill you need to improve on to avoid such occurrences in the future. Perhaps, you need to sharpen the way you run a meeting or your email instructions to a subordinate need to be clearer. Here is your chance to work on the skill. It might be as easy as being aware of the situation so that you do not repeat it. It could also mean enrolling in a course or looking for help to develop a certain skill or skillset. Indeed, the only place here where you are going to do yourself a disservice is if you know that you are deficient in some area that is necessary for you to do your job successfully and you do nothing about it!

Any good supervisor is going to realize this is going to happen to someone at one time or another. If they are on their game, they will use those occasions as a learning experience for the employee experiencing a setback or something going wrong. I say this in the hope that you have such a supervisor in your life as well as encouraging you to be that type of manager to your people.

When you are in a supervisory position to others, you have two obligations. They are to meet the goals of your job and to help those under you to become better at what they do. The truth is that these are not separate obligations but are intertwined together. A good manager knows that if they work to develop good people under them, then the manager's goals are going to be more easily met. This means not only accepting how people under you mess up, but working with them so that they learn from the experience and understand how to avoid doing it again in the future.

One of the ways a new manager usually messes up is by not working closely enough with their staff. If a subordinate does something wrong, then the supervisor might have missed doing something on his or her end that could have avoided the mess. In such a case, everyone learns something new in order to do better in the future.

We all like nothing better than to have our jobs move steadily upward toward success. That is not going to happen. There are always going to be peaks and valleys. That's okay. It is how we achieve that sought for "experience" that is going to put us in a good position to achieve our next promotion. The important thing is to be always mindful and present where we are now. When we mess up and turn it into a positive, then we grow and move forward. I once had one of my Chancellors, now retired, tell us at a staff meeting that we needed to go to places where others didn't want to go. It took me a minute to understand that, but I came to realize that it meant if we were going to do our jobs successfully, we needed to get out of our comfort zone and accept new challenges. Those new challenges were going to line the path to our next promotion. The unknown is always scary. In a job, encountering new tasks means new opportunities to mess up. Don't let that be a deterrent. If you mess up, then it was by trying something new. All this means is that you have an opportunity to learn something new and have that much more to put into your experience trunk!

It is important to know yourself in these situations. Self-awareness is the vital trait you need to mess up constructively. If you cannot be honest with a self-evaluation when something goes wrong, you are not going to have any positive outcome at all from the experience. You know the person that always blames something going wrong on someone else? Eventually, they are going to reach a point in their career where they either do not go any further or regress down the career ladder. It is not a sustainable position a person can place themselves in for their career. With that attitude, an individual is not going to learn from mistakes. He or she is probably going to have a revolving door on their department as they go through people by either constantly blaming them for problems or not helping them get better at their jobs. A manager such as this will eventually wear down his or her own supervisor.

From my coaching perspective, I've helped people navigate the aftermath of messing up in the workplace. I did it as part of my job or in support of a colleague and began coaching professionally in 2013. When you want to help others, it is a matter of being mindful. You have to be totally aware and in the present, as you listen to the other person. Then you can ask pertinent questions that probe deeper into the matter to find the root cause of the situation. As a coach, I have to be client-focused and centered on their agenda. I always have to keep in mind that this is their situation they are trying to learn from, not mine.

I once had a supervisor who told me there was a person in my unit that needed some help because the path that they were on was not a positive one. This individual was clashing with a faculty member. I realized that I could only help this person through coaching. At first, she wasn't sure what coaching was about, and I explained that it was a process to move forward both in their current position and with an eye to what their next career step would be. As we started meeting regularly, I learned that she was not very happy in her current job and wanted to move forward.

When working with someone, you help them see there are usually two paths that they can follow. One is true and deep, while the other is kind of superficial. The superficial one is like a band aid used to stop the flow of blood. It is first aid. The path of true and deep will lead to solid, long-term resolution. This person wanted to work on the long-term aspects of her career so we set about identifying her skillset strengths and matched them to a job that would be a better fit for her. The interesting part of the process is that she discovered skills that she did not realize she possessed.

She then applied for jobs that matched her expanded skillset. She was still hesitant, but when the opportunity came to be interviewed for one of them, she jumped at it. Lo and behold, she got the job!

Summary

There are times a person will need to mess up before they do a self-analysis of what they are good at and what skills need work. Coaching can help with this process, of course, but by whatever means a person gets to the solution point, that epiphany of discovery is a golden moment. When a person understands themselves better after messing up, then the newly learned lessons will help them in their current position and any promotion. Looking at it, it makes the learning experience worth it.

Complete the following sections for **"Management by Messing Up"** as it applies to your situation or career trajectory.

REFLECTION:

How can you use what you've learned in this chapter to change or improve the current situation? How can you apply what you've learned for career advancement? Hint: You can request support from a friend, colleague, mentor to assist you!

_____
_____
_____
_____
_____
_____
_____
_____
_____
_____
_____
_____
_____
_____
_____
_____
_____
_____
_____
_____
_____
_____
_____

ACTION STEPS:

List 1 or 2 action steps you intend to take starting today.

_____
_____
_____
_____
_____
_____
_____
_____
_____
_____
_____
_____
_____
_____
_____
_____
_____
_____
_____
_____
_____
_____
_____
_____

ACTION CELEBRATION:

After completing the actions over a couple of weeks, celebrate yourself. Write down how you will celebrate. Hint: It could be as small as listening to your favorite song, watching a favorite TV show, going out for dinner or...

_____

_____

_____

_____

_____

_____

_____

_____

_____

_____

_____

_____

_____

_____

_____

_____

_____

_____

_____

_____

_____

_____

I believe being a good time manager equates to being a successful leader.

CHAPTER 6

Time Management

❖ ❖ ❖ ❖ ❖ ❖ ❖

Felicia's cell phone rang as she was trying to put the finishing touches on a report so she could get out the door for a staff meeting. She picked it up and distractedly said, "Hello?"

"Hi, Felicia, I wanted to make sure you are coming tonight?"

Focusing back on the phone, Felicia asked, "Who is this?"

There was a moment of silence. Then a testy voice said, "It's your mother."

A flood of anxiety swept over Felicia. She took a quick look at the calendar and slumped in her chair. Steeling herself, she said, "Hi, Mom. Sorry, I was in the middle of something."

"I know my girl is busy at the university," her mother breezily said. "It's okay. I was making sure that you are coming over for your dad's birthday tonight."

"Um, I might have a little trouble making it," said Felicia. "I have to go to a recruitment at a high school tonight. If I get to your house, it might be kind of late," she finished lamely.

Another wave of silence greeted her on the phone. Finally, her mom said, "Felicia, I told you about this party a month ago. You said you would make sure that you would be there." There was a loud sigh on the phone. "Okay, I'll save you some cake. Please at least call your father at some point today." Before she could answer, her mother hung up.

Felicia stared at the quiet cell phone. It was her turn to sigh. She figured if there were 30 hours in a day, she still wouldn't have enough time to do everything she wanted. Looking at the clock, she saw she was five minutes late for the staff meeting. She got up, leaving the report unfinished on her laptop. That was already a day late, so what were a few more hours going to matter?

I am sure we are all familiar with the scenario above. Time is one of the more precious commodities. It is always constant, and it cannot be stored away to use for another day. We have to use it wisely, or we find it escaping our grasp quicker than a slippery watermelon seed. How often when you are fighting a deadline do you have that image in your head of the last grain of sand slipping into the bottom of the hourglass? Whenever that happens, you are now officially late!

The battle with time is more than completing one task in time. Unless approached properly, most people look at time as a battlefield where you have to go from one skirmish to another in order to reach the peacefulness when the battle is done. In the context of time, the battlefield is your day, and that peacefulness is when you finish work or go to sleep. Even there, you might not escape since all the situations you are dealing with during the day might invade your dreams.

Those daily skirmishes you encounter seem to increase in frequency and scope with our world's ever-changing technology. Advanced communications and computing speeds were supposed to make work easier. They certainly did on one level, but they also created an entirely new level of "I want it now!" With speed and efficiency comes an expectation of people doing their job faster and better. If you do not manage your time properly, your life becomes bogged down in meeting other people's expectations, which may or may not be your own.

I believe being a good time manager equates to being a successful leader. Several years ago, I did a pilot project with some faculty members because I saw an important need. Any good organization is going to give a new hire an orientation about the organization and go over its mission, expectations of employees, and goals for the future. Part of that orientation is explaining how the person's job fits into making all that the organization wants to achieve possible. What I observed to be missing was how the new staff member was going to arrange their time so that it was possible to meet all those goals and still have time for their personal life. What makes this concept even more difficult to get a handle on is that we are all at different points in our personal lives.

I remember that after I drew up a coaching contract with the school, the first employee who showed up came in with their hair tussled and breathing heavy as if they just completed a race. My first response was for them to take a seat and calm down. The person said, "You know, that's my number one objective. I don't know how to calm down and manage my time. I'm trying to do my work schedule and have some time and energy left for my students."

When I asked this young woman, and it could easily have been Felicia in the opening story, how much time she gave to her personal life, she only laughed. I knew what I wanted to accomplish in this project, but I never thought I would have such a textbook case of someone dealing with time management as my first participant.

I told the woman to put both feet on the floor, and take some time to breathe in deeply and relax. It took a little coaxing, but soon I could see her visibly relax. I then told her that there was no judgment in this room and the focus was on her getting more organized to be productive in her job and not feel as if she was constantly working. From there, we started to prioritize all that she had to do at work and in her life. This was not something that occurred in one meeting. We met several times as we focused on how she could organize and prioritize her time.

About a year and a half later, she was coming up on her tenure review. This is a college practice when a person is trying to become an associate or full professor at a university. My time management participant acknowledged that having those moments to become calm, relax, and focus on prioritizing what she needed to do helped her achieve a successful tenure position.

Based on her and other people I worked with, I felt like it was a success for me because I showed that giving people the time to mindfully think how they organized their time and duties was instrumental in achieving success in their position, as well as having a more balanced life between work and everything else. The irony here is that we get so bogged down in trying to fit everything into our time parameters that we rarely take the time to think our day through so that we can make the most of it. We need to force ourselves to take some time so that we can figure out the best way for us to utilize our time, rather than letting time control us.

To make time work for you is to adhere to a process of setting your goals and then to map out how you are going to achieve them. You can take the time of actually visualizing how you are going to accomplish something. In that visualization, you can break the accomplishment down into individual tasks and place them on the calendar. By taking this step, you can take the macro view of what you want to accomplish and can systematically go through all the micro steps needed to get there. It isn't a bad thing to force yourself to stop and think through a problem or goal. By taking a little time now to plan out things properly, you are saving yourself a lot of time later.

A quick word here about calendars. Use yours! It doesn't matter if it is the calendar on your smartphone or the old-fashioned kind. Tasks listed on a calendar mean nothing if you do not adhere to them. By this, I don't mean I want you to be a slave to your calendar. I don't want you to get uptight if there are things you didn't get to on any given day. That isn't very helpful. Rather, I want you to work at finding that fine line of sticking to your calendar but realizing that you can move some things to another day. This is where your ability to prioritize comes into play. Work on your priorities first every day. When you get them out of the way, you will be surprised how much more you can accomplish with your other tasks.

You don't want to beat yourself up for those things you don't get done by a certain day, week, or month. Keep working at them. It's okay if you don't get everything done. Say you have ten major goals for the week. If you've got seven or eight of them done, that's how many less you have to deal with tomorrow. However, if you didn't take the time to think through what you need to do and write them down, you would never have gotten that many accomplished!

A common symptom of having time control you instead of the other way around is procrastination. My new slogan is Nike's old one: "Just do it!" Overcoming procrastination has a lot to do with self-momentum. A huge cruise ship takes a long time to get up to full speed. When it does, there is no stopping it in the open ocean. That is how you can best deal with procrastination. If you have been putting off doing a bunch of things, make yourself get one of them done. Then pat yourself on the back and celebrate. Once you do that one thing, then maybe the next day or the next week or the next month you can do two or three things. If it is a big project, do the first item you need to do to start off, and feel good about it. Once we seem to do that one thing, then it seems easier to slowly incorporate other "to-dos" from our list and move forward. The momentum builds, and procrastination becomes a problem of the past.

When it comes to prioritizing, the list can be comprehensive, meaning it contains elements for both your personal and work life. Today, it is difficult to separate the two. Many jobs take a great deal of our time, but that doesn't mean you should have to sacrifice your personal time. To help balance out the Ying and Yang of your life, have one list and prioritize accordingly. Important family occasions and events deserve to be a high priority. Why else are you working so hard if you cannot enjoy your loved ones?

Practical personal matters also need to be high on your list. If you don't like the dentist, it is easy to substitute a meeting for a dentist appointment and justify it by saying work takes priority. It is hard to work if you have a problem with your mouth down the road or any other medical issue for that matter. Taking care of yourself is the number one priority, or the rest of your list has no meaning in the long run!

I once heard a time management expert say that when prioritizing, put the things that mean the most to you at the top of the list. This would be things like birthdays, anniversaries, or maybe that charity event you help at and go to every year. He also stressed to write down personal time for whatever is important to you — time at the gym, take a walk, sit down to read for fun, etc. You can't go crazy with this as we could all fill our days with fun stuff, but list enough of what helps you recharge your batteries and stay sharp. By taking care of ourselves, we are in a better position to perform well in our jobs.

Summary

Time is one of our most valuable resources, and we need to use it wisely. It is the one resource that cannot be saved, borrowed, or stopped. There are really only two ways to look at time — whether we let time control us or we successfully navigate it to get the most out of each day. That does not just happen. It takes discipline, and with no pun intended, time. If we take a little time to manage our time, we will find ourselves accomplishing more in our life with a lot less stress.

*Complete the following sections for **"Time Management"** as it applies to your situation or career trajectory.*

REFLECTION:

How can you use what you've learned in this chapter to change or improve the current situation? How can you apply what you've learned for career advancement? Hint: You can request support from a friend, colleague, mentor to assist you!

_____

_____

_____

_____

_____

_____

_____

_____

_____

_____

_____

_____

_____

_____

_____

_____

_____

_____

_____

_____

_____

_____

_____

_____

_____

ACTION STEPS:

List 1 or 2 action steps you intend to take starting today.

_____
_____
_____
_____
_____
_____
_____
_____
_____
_____
_____
_____
_____
_____
_____
_____
_____
_____
_____
_____
_____
_____
_____
_____
_____

ACTION CELEBRATION:

After completing the actions over a couple of weeks, celebrate yourself. Write down how you will celebrate. Hint: It could be as small as listening to your favorite song, watching a favorite TV show, going out for dinner or...

_____
_____
_____
_____
_____
_____
_____
_____
_____
_____
_____
_____
_____
_____
_____
_____
_____
_____
_____
_____
_____

To me, one of the wonders of life is never knowing what is around the corner.

CHAPTER 7

Life Happens

❖ ❖ ❖ ❖ ❖ ❖ ❖ ❖

A s snow fell gently over the campus, Trey hurried to his office. This was his first time back since the semester break started. He had some fun over the Christmas holidays and felt recharged for the new semester. He liked being a TA and thought it was good training for when he started teaching at a college after he finished his degree. The financial break it gave him on his tuition made his master's program affordable. Now that he had his first semester behind him, he looked forward to being more comfortable during this one.

As he entered the building, he noticed construction equipment and the strong smell of paint permeating the air. As he rounded the corner in the hallway to his department, he stopped and stared. Where there used to be offices, framework stood waiting for walls to be put up. Part of him realized that the floor looked big without any walls. Another part wondered if he missed the memo that they were gutting his department.

Linda, one of the department's administrative assistants, entered the room. She smiled at Trey's surprised look and said, "Don't worry, they didn't tell any of us. The Facilities Department scheduled the upgrade and forgot to tell all of us who work here. We are now crammed over in Silas Hall. Also, Professor Watson decided to take a sabbatical while on break, so she is not back. Rachael, the other TA, decided *to transfer, so you are also picking up her classes this semester. Oh, and financial aid said to give them a call. There seems to be something wrong with your aid package."*

Trey wondered if it was too late to go home and back to bed, with the sheets over his head.

You can become the most accomplished time management expert in the world, but life has a way of throwing you curveball after curveball to get you off your game. To me, one of the wonders of life is never knowing what is around the corner. Conversely, one of the banes of life is never knowing what is around the corner!

It is wonderful to have a plan and stick to it, but no plan can allow for every contingency. I am an advocate for visualizing and mapping out a course for your job, your career, and your life, but at the same time, I will tell you not to engrave that plan in stone. You need to keep a fluidity around all of your strategies so that you can exercise flexibility and make adjustments on the fly. Think of your plans as a firm guideline rather than hard and fast rules.

In the story that introduces the chapter, Trey has what can be termed a bad day. You come into work enthused and ready to hit the floor running and things go to hell before you get your coat off. In the grand scheme of things, his obstacles aren't life-changing, but he has to bounce with the punches. I also want to point out that good things happen in life that can also throw your best laid plans out the window. The point is to approach your work, career, and life with the mindset that not everything is going to go according to plan.

I lived through a transition when I went from the military to civilian work. I hadn't completed my degree yet, but I found a good job and I was pretty comfortable with myself. Then life happened. The company I was with downsized and I was laid off. I didn't have the degree that I felt I needed. The short version is that I was unemployed. If nothing else, you know I speak here from experience.

However, I resolved to stick to my guns, which meant obtaining my degree and getting the job I wanted. I went back to school and started a salaried job where my time was not determined by set hours. That usually means you work more than an eight-hour day, so I was doing that while juggling schoolwork. I had a professor who stated the obvious when he said, "Life happens," when he heard what I had been through. Not particularly helpful, but it did resonate with me.

When life happens, you have to make the best of it. If that means acquiring new skills or advanced education to get the job you want, then so be it. You have three choices when faced with obstacles in life. You can whine and do nothing about your situation. You can whine and pursue a course of action to get you out of the situation. You can quietly do what you need to do to get out of your situation. The second and third choices have the same result, but the third choice is much more gracious and dignified!

The optimal course of action is to be proactive when life throws you obstacles. I knew someone who worked at a company, and he saw the signs six months before the doors closed at the business. He used that time to set up his own business that he always wanted and effortlessly slid into that the day he was given his pink slip. I was proactive in how I pursued my career, but then life reared its head again. I was diagnosed with anemia, and the doctor told me that he wasn't sure why I was still alive or what was going on with me. One thing about that type of news is that it put a career change in perspective. It is important, but not as important as your health. I did the treatment that I had to do and kept plugging forward.

There are a couple of lessons I learned as a result of working on my health, school, and a job at the same time. For me, I am a believer, and I think having a belief in a higher power is a good anchor to have when life goes upside down. The other thing I discovered is that I learned that we are so busy, busy, busy that we don't rest. We need to take that time out to refocus ourselves on everything we are doing. In this instance, I was forced to rest. Now I voluntarily force myself to rest and use that time to make sure I have a good balance with what I am doing in my life.

When I was going through that period of my life, I began to implement a process of trusting and believing in myself. I recognized that my life had something important to offer others. This helped me to strengthen my personal resolve and to move forward. That attitude has thrust me to where I am today because I decided that I was not going to coast through life. I knew there would always be obstacles, difficulties, and challenges. If I could get through that period of my life, I felt that my process would see me through any setbacks in my future. As I developed that tenacity, it served as a foundation for everything that came after.

Developing trust in others is hard. I think it is even more difficult to trust yourself! If I were to define how to trust yourself, the complex part of it is actually going through the process and understanding that people will recognize your efforts. This recognition is an acknowledgment that what you are doing is worth it. In a career situation, when you are trusting yourself that you are doing your best to do your job and to improve, you will receive positive signs from subordinates, peers, and superiors. This positive re-enforcement will be an encouragement that you are on the right track and to continue doing your best. While it might not necessarily lead to a promotion right away, it will happen. Trust in your own process that it is going to take you to where you are meant to be as a leader.

Setbacks allow you to provide a story for the next person, so they can move forward and gain inspiration from your efforts. That is the ultimate purpose of this book. Your example of how to handle adversity is going to have an impact on others whether it is an employee, colleague, family member, or friend. It comes down to trusting yourself and having trust in life. Sometimes when we have our goals and dreams, we don't achieve them right away. As you adjust to what you are doing so that discouragement does not stop you, others will cheer you on and find inspiration by what you do. You don't know when you are giving a push to someone else getting back on track to fulfill their dreams after encountering obstacles.

From a job perspective, you went through the job hunting and interview process and landed your job. You have to remember that you only came into contact with a small number of folks from the organization that now employs you. They are the only ones who know you. When you start your first day of work, others need to see why you were hired. It is not a job interview all over again, but you have to trust in yourself that you can show other people why you have the job. Here, job performance is going to speak louder than words. Be open and honest in all that you do. Use some of the ideas I talked about in this book. As with your interview, go to work each day with a sense of mindfulness. Be totally aware of the moment you are in, and get the most out of each day.

In your first hundred days, foster as many helpful relationships as you can. Sort out who you can learn from and any individuals who might bring a toxic environment to the workplace. Be proactive where you can in your job. If you go to meetings and do not have anything to offer yet when you are new, take notes. I always have a goal to find at least one new piece of information at a meeting that I didn't know before.

Take note of what skill sets you possess that help you with your job and what new ones you must work on. Know where your organization is going and how you fit into that picture. By all means, be honest. Don't act like you know everything when you don't. Even when you have time in the job under your belt and you are asked a question that you don't have an answer for, it is okay to say, "I don't know, but I will find out as soon as possible and get back to you with an answer." Doing that draws the respect of others as opposed to making stuff up!

What you are doing when you enter a new position mindfully and honestly is to prepare yourself when life lets loose with some surprises. You are laying a foundation for yourself as a person and in your job by trying to do everything correctly. Athletes and actors have something in common. They repeat over and over everything they are going to do in a game or in a performance. While their goal is to do their job flawlessly, the work they do beforehand prepares them to adapt to a situation when things go wrong. An athlete can recover quickly if knocked off the execution of their sport. A trained actor can instinctively work around someone missing their lines or a piece of scenery falling in the middle of a performance. It is the work they put in and the trust they have in themselves that makes this possible.

That is the attitude we all need to take into our jobs. While nobody likes life to take an unexpected turn, we want to be ready when it does. Everybody has it in them to take the necessary steps to be ready when life happens. The trick is to start preparing for that moment now. After all, we do not know when it will occur!

Summary

"Man plans, God laughs." This is an old Yiddish saying that has validity in our day-to-day existence. We never know what tomorrow will bring. We have to move forward as if our plan is going to be flawless, but we have to be ready to pivot when things go wrong. Being ready for any eventuality is impossible. However, it is possible to prepare yourself to handle any obstacles. It is not so much about having a list of contingency plans but using what you have already done in life to weather any oncoming storms. Ultimately, it seems to be how we navigate a storm that will define us.

Complete the following sections for *"**Life Happens**"* as it applies to your situation or career trajectory.

REFLECTION:

How can you use what you've learned in this chapter to change or improve the current situation? How can you apply what you've learned for career advancement? Hint: You can request support from a friend, colleague, mentor to assist you!

_____

_____

_____

_____

_____

_____

_____

_____

_____

_____

_____

_____

_____

_____

_____

_____

_____

_____

_____

_____

_____

_____

_____

_____

_____

ACTION STEPS:

List 1 or 2 action steps you intend to take starting today.

_____
_____
_____
_____
_____
_____
_____
_____
_____
_____
_____
_____
_____
_____
_____
_____
_____
_____
_____
_____
_____
_____
_____
_____
_____
_____
_____

ACTION CELEBRATION:

After completing the actions over a couple of weeks, celebrate yourself. Write down how you will celebrate. Hint: It could be as small as listening to your favorite song, watching a favorite TV show, going out for dinner or...

You cannot prevent everything from happening that will throw a plan off. What you can do is develop the skill to adjust quickly to something going wrong.

CHAPTER 8

Putting It Together

❖ ❖ ❖ ❖ ❖ ❖ ❖

F ive years later, Felicia entered her new office at the biggest university in the state. The selection committee had been deadlocked on choosing Felicia or another applicant for this position. At the deciding interview, the committee had thrown various scenarios at Felicia to see how she would handle such situations. While she had not directly encountered all of them in her career so far, there were enough similarities to things she did face that she was able to draw on that experience and effectively explain what she would do in each case. Her responses were the deciding factor for the committee and now she was here on her first day. She decided to spend this day talking to her supervisor and meet as many people as she could with whom she would be working closely. She took one more look at her calendar to make sure she was on schedule and got started.

On the same campus, Trey walked over to his advisor for the doctorate program. He received his master's several years ago and enjoyed the teaching he was doing at the community college. However, about a year ago, he realized he missed the challenge and atmosphere of a big college. That thought made him research doctorate programs and what he needed to do to teach and work at a university. Those lessons he learned as a TA served him well as he started to juggle his teaching with his doctorate studies. He was confident of his dissertation topic and was going to his advisor to finalize the concept. Looking around *the square he was in, Trey could visualize walking these grounds or similar ones very soon with the title of "Professor."*

We covered different topics to help you navigate the interview process as you look for a position in academia and some of the skills necessary to excel in your newfound position. The foundation for everything I talked about is to have a foundation of mindfulness and to be present in the moment. You always need to be cognizant of what is going on in the environment around you whether you're in an interview, a meeting, or talking one-on-one with a colleague. When you are mindful in all situations, you comprehend what is going on, and you are in a better position to then make good decisions. By becoming so adept at exercising mindfulness that it becomes a natural part of who you are, you place yourself in a good position of projecting yourself to the next level of your career.

It all starts with you understanding and realizing what skill sets and traits you bring to a position. We often have an instinctive feel for what we can contribute to a position, but we never take the time to think them through thoroughly. It is well worth the time to review your abilities and list them. Abilities are everything from the technical knowledge you need to perform the job you want, to other abilities such as a proclivity for organization or motivating people. There is nothing wrong with listing the traits you have and those that you believe you lack. It will enable you to better match up to a position where you think you will fit, as well as showing you where you need to do some work on self-improvement.

As you go into an interview for a position: prepare, prepare, prepare! You need to know yourself and the school where you are interviewing. This way, you can present yourself as the best fit for the school. You can be the school's "problem solver," or at least the best person to solve any problems your position requires you to deal with. This is the mindset you want when you go into any interview. If you don't get the job, at least learn from the interview. Whether it was a matter of not preparing enough or not feeling comfortable with answering certain questions, take that information back with you and apply it to your next interview. Remember, every interview is a learning experience that will make you more prepared the next time.

Since mindfulness is so much a part of success in an interview, your job, your career, and your life, it is worth reviewing the concept in some detail here. Even when you believe mindfulness is an inherent part of your life, it never hurts to go back and familiarize yourself with what it is. Sometimes it helps to return to fundamentals, especially if you find yourself off track a little.

As you know, mindfulness means being completely in the moment and aware of everything happening around you. It takes a conscious effort to become mindful. By constantly being aware of being mindful and applying yourself to its practice every day, it will soon become a part of you. The hardest part of mindfulness is when you are attempting to use it when relating with other people. When you use the nonjudgement filters of mindfulness, you can focus better on who the other person you are trying to talk to is, and what he or she is trying to communicate with you.

Mindfulness is important if you are a Millennial or you work with them. As you recall, this category encompasses all those between 22 and 37 years old. They enter the workforce with a great education and the resources and knowledge to navigate an accelerated career path. On the other hand, they have a hard time grasping the practicalities of a new job so that they can excel in their position. As a group, they also have difficulty adapting and working within the rules of wherever they are employed.

As a Millennial, you have to learn how to be successful within the context of where your job is. If you are of an older generation who works with the younger, then this is a skill set you want to teach them. The valuable lesson you want Millennials to learn is that a person has to know what has been done in the past where they are working and what the future goals of the organization are. Using that knowledge and continually using the experience they acquire every day will help them plan their accomplishments. Millennials who can combine their education and technical know-how with an understanding of who they work for will go very far in their career.

Of course, any career can be slowed down when working in a toxic environment. Identifying the sources of that toxic environment is not always easy. When a person is publicly outspoken and shows their negative inclinations, it is easy to recognize the source of trouble. However, other people project negativity in subtler ways. Here is where you need to look at the micro-aggressive behavior of people. These tend to be small, casual verbal and behavioral slights against any person or group.

Through observation, you can tell when a person has something against an individual or a certain group of people based on age, race, religion, etc. Micro-aggressive behavior can be anything from making a sneer when someone is talking or a more public display of opposition when in a meeting. You can also gather micro-aggressive tendencies from how someone words an email or how a person interacts with you.

It takes a mindful observation on your part to spot these micro-aggressions. You do have a responsibility to deal with it, both for yourself and the sake of the workplace. Micro-aggressive behavior can gather momentum in a way that ratchets up the toxic environment in the workplace. Depending on your position, do what you can to halt such behavior.

One of my favorite concepts is reminding you that there are going to be times when you mess up something while you are doing your job. It is going to happen more than once too; I can tell you that. Nobody is perfect, and there are going to be situations that arise where the initial decision you make might not be the best one and lead to chaos, or at least an uncomfortable situation. The trick here, as in everything you do, is to learn from the situation.

When you figure out how you might have done better to avoid messing up, you must focus on whatever you did incorrectly. You could see what skill you need to improve on to avoid such occurrences in the future. Here is your opportunity to acquire or improve on that skill. You are only going to do yourself a disservice if you know that you are deficient in some area that is necessary for you to do your job successfully and you don't act on it.

I think if I had to rate the most important topic I discussed in this book, it is time management. It is the one thing that we never seem to have enough of, and nobody is ever going to make the day longer than 24 hours. Therefore, we have to work within that 24-hour constraint. In reality, it is less than that, as scientists are constantly finding new reasons why sleep is so important to our well-being.

To make time work for you is to adhere to a process of setting your goals and then to map out how you are going to achieve them. You can then break down those accomplishments into the individual tasks needed to bring them to fruition and place them on your calendar. It is beneficial to make yourself stop and think through a problem or goal. By taking a little time now to plan out things properly, you are saving yourself a lot of time later.

There are many processes and tools to help you become a competent time manager. You can search the internet, take a course, or use any number of systems. The one thing you cannot do is avoid doing anything about improving your time management skills because you claim that you "don't have any time!"

No matter how good you become with mindfulness, directing Millennials, and exercising great time management skills, remember that life is full of unknowns. "The best-laid plans of mice and men often go awry. No matter how carefully a project is planned, something may still go wrong with it." The saying is adapted from a line in "To a Mouse," by Robert Burns. It is a reminder that no matter how much time and effort goes into a plan, life can throw out the random obstacle that screws up the entire concept.

You cannot prevent everything from happening that will throw a plan off. What you can do is develop the skill to adjust quickly to something going wrong. This comes with experience. Mindfulness comes into play here as you need to be aware of what is going on around you when the unexpected occurs. That is the first step that allows you to evaluate the situation and come up with remedies to solve it. The important thing is not to let the negatives that come at you throw you off. Accept them, shake them off, and get to work making a bad situation better.

Unfortunately, you will have plenty of chances to refine this skill. The randomness of life keeps us on our toes; at least, it should. As with everything else we talked about, be mindful of using any event as a learning situation. Yes, you will run into unique situations every now and then. However, as your career spreads over time, you will encounter obstacles that will have a similarity to past experiences. Use those experiences to guide you through the new situation.

I think that is a good maxim to end this book. Apply the principles I share here but be mindful of using your experiences to guide you in the future. In all that I talk about here, be mindful of how to apply them to your career and life. As time goes on, you will garner more experience in so many diverse areas that you can fall back on those experiences to help guide you. In everything you do, learn for the future.

Complete the following sections for *"**Putting it Together**"* as it applies to your situation or career trajectory.

REFLECTION:

How can you use what you've learned in this chapter to change or improve the current situation? How can you apply what you've learned for career advancement? Hint: You can request support from a friend, colleague, mentor to assist you!

_____

_____

_____

_____

_____

_____

_____

_____

_____

_____

_____

_____

_____

_____

_____

_____

_____

_____

_____

_____

_____

_____

_____

_____

ACTION STEPS:

List 1 or 2 action steps you intend to take starting today.

_____
_____
_____
_____
_____
_____
_____
_____
_____
_____
_____
_____
_____
_____
_____
_____
_____
_____
_____
_____
_____
_____
_____
_____
_____

ACTION CELEBRATION:

After completing the actions over a couple of weeks, celebrate yourself. Write down how you will celebrate. Hint: It could be as small as listening to your favorite song, watching a favorite TV show, going out for dinner or...

_____

_____

_____

_____

_____

_____

_____

_____

_____

_____

_____

_____

_____

_____

_____

_____

_____

_____

_____

_____

_____

_____

www.ingramcontent.com/pod-product-compliance
Lightning Source LLC
LaVergne TN
LVHW011336080426
835513LV00006B/385